FINANCIAL COUNSELING & ACCESS FOR THE FINANCIALLY VULNERABLE

Findings from the Assessing Financial Capability Outcomes (AFCO) Adult Pilot

cfed
expanding economic opportunity

April 2014

This report was prepared by the Corporation for Enterprise Development (CFED) under contract TOS-11-F-039 for the U.S. Department of the Treasury.

Authors

Kasey Wiedrich	CFED
Nathalie Gons	NYC Department of Consumer Affairs Office of Financial Empowerment
J. Michael Collins	Center for Financial Security, University of Wisconsin-Madison
Anita Drever	CFED

Acknowledgements

This pilot would not have been possible without the contributions and cooperation of Amelia Erwitt and Monica Copeland from the New York City Department of Consumer Affairs Office of Financial Empowerment, the New York City Parks Opportunity Program and Popular Community Bank (formerly Banco Popular). Michael Batty, and Karen Walsh from UW-Madison and Kerry Griffin provide invaluable research assistance. Thank you also to Ida Rademacher and Leigh Tivol from CFED for their guidance and input throughout the design and implementation of the pilot and the drafting of the findings and implications.

We would also like to thank the following representatives from the organizations involved in the implementation of the AFCO pilot for their cooperation in this research and for taking the time to share with us their experiences with the pilot.

New York City Department of Parks & Recreation, Parks Opportunity Program
- Elizabeth Ehrlich, Chief, Parks Opportunity Program
- Davida Rowley, Supervisor of Client Services, Division of Education and Training

Popular Community Bank
- Brian Doran, Region Executive, New York Metro Region & Director of Governmental Affairs
- Dawn M. Carrillo, Vice President, NY Metro Marketing Manager
- Wendy Scarlett, Vice President, former Branch Manager

New York City Financial Empowerment Center Counselors
- Pedro Salazar, Phipps Community Development Corporation
- Joseph Frewer, Neighborhood Trust Financial Partners
- Adalberto Jaimes, Neighborhood Trust Financial Partners

DEPARTMENT OF THE TREASURY
WASHINGTON, D.C. 20220

April, 2014

Dear Colleagues:

The Department of the Treasury is pleased to have commissioned this report on leveraging financial counseling and financial access to improve unbanked Americans' financial capability. The research, conducted over two years, takes a rigorous look at two important strategies – access to a transaction account and financial counseling – that hold promise to help a population of particularly vulnerable Americans better manage their financial resources and move up the economic ladder.

These important findings will inform Treasury's work and the work of other agencies across government, as well as the efforts of the private and non-profit sectors, as we all seek to build the financial capability of Americans so they are better prepared to fully participate in our nation's economy.

We are very pleased to have worked with CFED, the Center for Financial Security of the University of Wisconsin-Madison, the City of New York's Office of Financial Empowerment, and the City of New York's Parks Opportunity Program in the design and implementation of the study, and we are grateful for the contributions of everyone involved in the project, including the study participants.

These findings will expand understanding of best practices as the Department considers policies to help working people manage their money, transition back into the workforce, and strive to move up the economic ladder. We will share the findings with the President's Advisory Council on Financial Capability for Young Americans, and our partner federal agencies in the Financial Literacy and Education Commission. Finally, we encourage policy makers across all levels of government, employers, financial institutions, advocacy organizations and social service providers to similarly use this assessment, and consider further research and evaluation of similar projects.

Best regards,

Melissa Koide
Deputy Assistant Secretary for Consumer Policy
U.S. Department of the Treasury

Contents

Introduction

Approximately one in twelve American households do not have a checking or savings account, and among very low-income households the proportion that is unbanked jumps to more than one in four.[1] Not only do these low-income households lack basic financial tools, but they may also need to build their financial capability—the ability to make informed decisions about the use and management of money. With support from the U.S. Department of the Treasury, Corporation for Enterprise Development (CFED), the Center for Financial Security at the University of Wisconsin-Madison (CFS), and the New York City Department of Consumer Affairs Office of Financial Empowerment (OFE) partnered on a pilot program to test the effect of paring of financial access and an average of one to two hours of financial counseling on the financial capability of a population transitioning off of public benefits in New York City. The Assessing Financial Capability Outcomes (AFCO) pilot study provides unique evidence of the causal effects of counseling provided through a public program.

Research suggests that the combination of financial education and financial access may improve financial knowledge, behavior, and outcomes (see Baker and Dylla [2007] for a review of some of these studies). However, research to-date largely examines the impacts of financial education and financial access as a single treatment, without attempts to untangle interactions or 'bundling' strategies. The AFCO pilot assesses the combined and separate impacts of financial access and counseling on the financial capability and well-being of unbanked adults. Financial counseling, which offers personalized assistance, seemed an appropriate intervention for a historically highly unbanked population.

The AFCO pilot was an effort to integrate financial empowerment services into an existing workforce program: the New York City Parks Opportunity Program (POP), a transitional employment program for adults moving off of public assistance. Adding financial empowerment services to a program already in place may improve the odds of both interventions' success.[2] Programs working with clients in financial transition such as welfare-to-work, transitional employment, domestic violence and prisoner re-entry programs may achieve stronger outcomes if their clients are given tools to better manage their money, improve their credit scores and plan their financial futures. Similarly, programs offering financial counseling and bank account access may

---

[1] Federal Deposit Insurance Corporation. (2012). *2011 FDIC National Survey of Unbanked and Underbanked Households.* http://www.fdic.gov/householdsurvey/2012_unbankedreport.pdf

[2] For more on the potential impact of an integrated services model see: The Annie E. Casey Foundation. 2010. "An Integrated Approach to Fostering Family Economic Success: How Three Model Sites are Implementing the Center for Working Families Approach." http://www.aecf.org/KnowledgeCenter/Publications.aspx?pubguid=%7BF0C4C227-E25E-4B20-A005-0DE98 2FA82C%7D., and Kovach, Andrea. 2009. "Integrating Asset-Building Strategies into Domestic Violence Advocacy." *Clearinghouse Review* 43 (148). http://drupaldev.povertylaw.org/sites/default/files/files/webinars/assets-dv/kovach.pdf.

also be more likely to have higher take-up if they are integrated into the structure or delivery systems of programs that clients trust.

POP participants represent a population that is underserved by mainstream financial services. A total of 1,034 POP participants took part in this study and were offered safe, affordable bank accounts with direct deposit. Just under half (49%) of the participants were also offered free financial counseling and paid time off from work to attend counseling. The remaining half of participants was not offered counseling through POP, but could still access counseling services in the community if they wished. Using this research design, this study examined the impact of financial counseling on:

- The general financial capability and well-being of participants, including credit history, financial behavior and financial attitudes;
- The use of a checking account.

Administrative data, credit reports and scores, self-report surveys and bank transaction data were collected at baseline and then six and 12 months following enrollment in the study. In addition, interviews with program stakeholders and POP participants were conducted to document the implementation of this pilot and examine how financial counseling and access can be successfully integrated into existing programs.

The primary finding of this study is that counseling clients are more likely to stay current on debt payments—specifically, access to financial counseling is associated with a lower percentage of debt that is past due 12 months after starting the POP program. This is an important outcome as it suggests the counseling services focused clients so they paid more attention to financial management, and these behaviors were maintained even after the counseling was completed. Paying bills on time is a leading indicator for improving credit history and ultimately credit access over the life course.[3] These findings are especially important given the high rates of unemployment, high debt and housing instability among the study population (see Appendix B for comparisons to national averages).

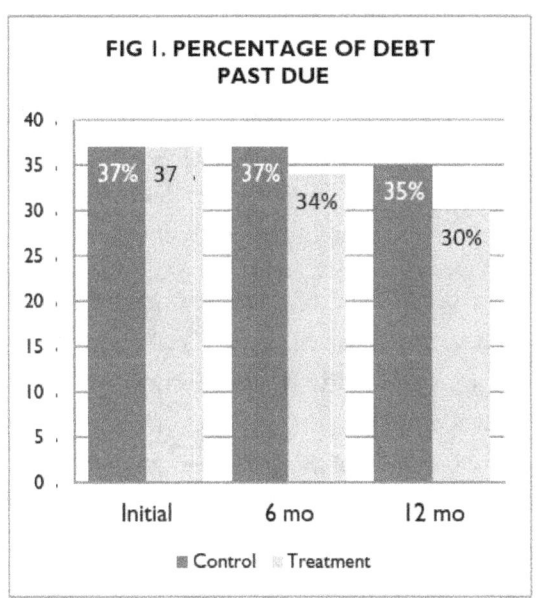

FIG I. PERCENTAGE OF DEBT PAST DUE

---

[3] According to the Fair Isaac Corporation, payment history contributes 35% to FICO score calculations for the general population, the largest of any component, including the amount owed (30%), length of credit history (15%), new credit (10%) and types of credit used (10%). For more information, see: http://www.myfico.com/CreditEducation/WhatsInYourScore.aspx

The data in this stu ly do not support statistically significa it improve ients in banking access or use that can be causally linked to access to financial counseli ig, althoug the overall rate of *all* POP participants being banked increased dramatically from about a third o over half. This project also helped t document range of perceived and actual barriers o enrolling in bank accounts, which may be instructive to other public and community-based programs.

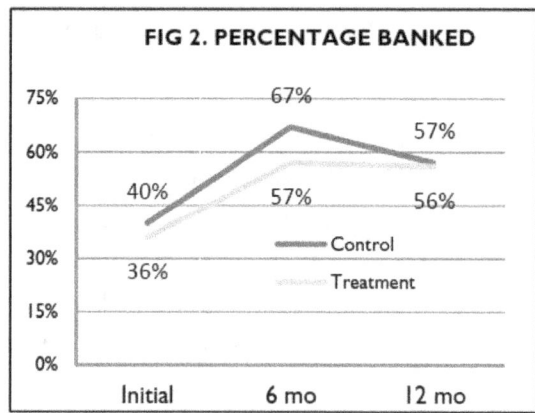

This stu ly offers a unique look at the financial lives of a population transitioning off of public benefits and addresses several of the research priorities identified by the Financial Literacy and Education Commissi n in 2012:

- I lentify and evaluate the relationship between fi ancial educ ition and access to and design of high quality financial products.
- Evaluate the delivery of financial education for youth an l adults in order to identify effective approaches, delivery channels, and other factors (such as the interaction of knowledge, products, and behaviors) that enhance effectiveness.
- I lentify, evaluate, and build consensus on "key metrics" for financial education/capability, i icluding me isures of knowledge, behavior, and well-being.
- I lentify opp rtunities and roles for local, state, and fed ral governments as scalable platforms for financial capability.

The rem under of thi paper is organized into the following sections: Section 2 provides an overview of the prior research on financial counseling and use of financial se vices, Section 3 describes the program and study lesign, Section 4 describes the data collected during the pilot and the sample analyzed in this report, Section 5 describes the research finding;, Section 6 summarizes the documentation of the implementation, and Section 7 offer insights for practice and policy.

Prior Studie

In the U ited States, there is general literature on financial counseli g that dates back to the early 1970s, much of which focuses on mortgage payment is ues (see Collins & O'Rourke, 2010, for a review). Many evalu itions are descriptive and lack a com parison group, or they compare clients to a non-ran om comparison group. For example, Elliehausen et al. (2007) evaluated the effects of credit counseli ig, comparing clients who received counseling to a non-rand m comparison group that did not parti ipate in co nseling. While the initial analysis indicated that counseling led to considerable improvements in credit scores three years after counseling, the estimated effects decreased sharply after controlling for which clients sought help. Other studies follow a similar pattern, largely due to a randomized design that allows for estimating causal effects of counseling.

Studies of workplace-based financial capability interventions have mainly focused on retirement planning and savings education seminars (Bernheim & Garrett, 2003; Bayer, Bernheim & Scholz, 2008). These studies are suggestive that employer-based financial education is associated with higher rates of participation and contribution rates for retirement accounts. But there have been no studies of workplace-based financial counseling on lower-income people related to basic household financial management outside of retirement savings.

No prior studies have examined the effects of counseling on being unbanked (defined as not having a checking or savings account). People may be unbanked due to restrictions such as unresolved overdrafts or unauthorized use (Barr, 2004; Romich et al. 2010), lack of accepted forms of personal identification (Fine, Leimbach, & Jacob, 2006) or because they either choose not to open an account or have not gotten around to opening an account. Some people do not have accounts due to the costs involved, while others are hampered by the perception that having formal savings could harm eligibility for public assistance programs (O'Brien, 2006) or could trigger collections judgments (Prescott & Tatar, 1999; O'Brien, 2012). Additionally, distrust of financial institutions and privacy concerns contribute to the individual's decision to remain unbanked (Barr & Sharraden, 2005). Unbanked households may find it more difficult to access or receive a line of credit relative to banked households, as lenders have limited means by which to determine creditworthiness (Agarwal et al., 2011). Without access to financial liquidity, people may become more vulnerable to unexpected negative income or expenditure shocks.

Direct deposit has been described as a "pre-commitment" constraint that converts a series of recurring, potentially difficult decisions into a single, perhaps easier, decision to use direct deposit (Beverly et al., 2003; Beverly et al., 2008). Not only may direct deposit reduce the temptation to spend "cash in hand," it also reduces the financial and time-related costs of making deposits personally (Bertrand et al., 2006). Offering direct deposit to participants could increase their awareness, understanding, and trust of direct deposit by providing experience with its use.

Overall, the financial capability strategies included in this study—financial (primarily credit-focused) counseling and access to low-fee transactional accounts, including an employer-supported direct deposit function—are discussed in prior studies as potentially being appropriate for POP employees. But few studies examine a population as financially distressed as POP participants, and none include a combination of counseling and banking access. Prior studies also lack a formalized quasi-experimental framework to facilitate a causal analysis of financial counseling. This study provides several unique potential contributions to the literature and ideally can serve as the foundation of new research on integrated financial capability and access focused in low-income and vulnerable populations.

Pilot Design and Implementation

POP is one of the nation's largest transitional employment program s. Administered by New York City's Department of Parks and Recreation, POP provides six months of full-time employment coupled with job sea ch counseling and other human cap tal enrichm nt activities to approximately 6,000 adults receivin ; public assistance annually. POP participants w rk in New York City's parks, playgrounds and recreation centers, with the goal of tr nsitioning to private sector employment. Through ut the program, POP participants gain transferable skills in fields such as security, horticult re, administration, maintenance and customer service while receiving employment services and career ounseling. Since its inception in 19 4, the training program has placed over 11,000 tr inees into f ll-time positions.

POP participants are heads of household who have been eceiving Temporary Assistance for Needy Families (TANF) at the time of POP enrollment. The New York City Human Resources Administration, the gency that administers the City's T NF progra n, refers eligible clients to the POP program who have been screened for "work-readiness," which includes screening for mental health a d substanc abuse issues, physical capability a d the abilit to take direction in English. During the six- month program, participants work 35 ours per w ek earning $9.21 an hour as employe s of the Parks Department. The participants' goal is to pr pare for, search for and find secure e nployment during the program, and transition from public assistance to self-sufficiency. Participants cycle th ough the program building their s ills in wee ly specialized vocational and job-readiness trainin . Participants may also enroll in education (GE), adult basic education, ESL) and com uter classes in preparation for private sector em loyment.

The Ne York City Department of Consumer Affairs Office of Financial Empowerment (OFE) manage the implementation of the research pilot and hired three for ner POP participants as "POP specialis s" to assist with the enrollment in and implementation of this study. Feedback from these former POP participants on what messages and real-life e amples resonated with them informed the script us d in the offer of bank accounts, financial counseling and th opportunity to participate in the stud to POP employees. Between January and early May 2012, t e POP specialists worked on-site at P P locations across four New York City boroug s[4] to enroll POP participants in the study and implement the p lot.

BANKING ACCESS

All participants enr lled in the study were offered checking accounts by a local bank, Popular Commu ity Bank (formerly Banco Popular). The accoun offered to participants is a 'safe' account

---

[4] One bor ugh – Staten sland – was excluded from this study in part because opular Community Bank does not have bran hes in that borough; this is also the smallest POP site a d was unlikely to provide enough client volume for the pu poses of the study.

with no direct marketing of an overdraft protection option, intended to protect participants from unintentionally incurring overdraft fees.[5] The accounts also had no minimum monthly balance requirement, and few other requirements (see Appendix C for the account terms). Popular Community Bank also agreed to provide flexibility in opening accounts for POP employees with past problems with a transaction account. In most cases, those with outstanding funds owed to another institution below $100 were forgiven. The bank also allowed employer letters with employee addresses to suffice as "proof of address," a requirement when opening an account. These flexibilities are an important feature of this program given the historically under-banked nature of the POP population.

During their POP orientation day, the POP specialists offered all POP employees Popular checking accounts and direct deposit of their City paychecks to either a bank account or prepaid card (if the participant already had a card). A Popular staff member was present on-site to facilitate the account opening and answer questions about the account and banking more generally. Participants received their account number that day and were able to fill out direct deposit forms while opening their accounts. At the bank branch following the opening on-site, the bank representative confirmed the individual's ability to open the account and notified the client by phone or letter in cases where account opening was not possible (for example, due to a negative ChexSystems report). All POP participants received basic information about direct deposit and account benefits and use.

Study participants who did not open an account with Popular at orientation were offered a second opportunity to open an account and enroll in direct deposit approximately two weeks later at a POP professional development day. At this second presentation, the POP specialists provided "light-touch" financial education focused on short term and long term financial goals, and again reviewed the terms of the Popular account. Popular staff was again on-site to answer questions and open accounts. At this second offer, all participants were offered a $25 incentive for enrolling in direct deposit, on to any type of account at any financial institution, not just the Popular accounts.

The response to the bank account and direct deposit offers was more enthusiastic than OFE and the Parks Department expected. A total of 55% of the total POP participants enrolled in the study signed up for direct deposit and 49% applied for a new checking account with Popular.[6] Prior to the implementation of the AFCO pilot, approximately 15 of POP participants enrolled in direct deposit. The high take up of accounts suggests unbanked participants had a strong desire to become banked when given access to an account with agreeable terms. However, even with the flexibility

---

[5] Without overdraft protection, point-of-sale purchases or ATM withdrawal requests were denied in the case of insufficient funds in the account, limiting the accrual of overdraft fees. However, there were instances when insufficient funds fees were applied.

[6] Take-up of direct deposit is higher than take-up of the Popular accounts as some participants that were previously banked signed up for direct deposit to their existing account (checking account or a prepaid card). Approximately one-third of the study sample had a bank account in the month prior to joining POP and 31% had a prepaid card in the month prior to POP.

Popular Community Bank providing in opening accounts through the pilot, approximately one-third of the participants who applied for a checking account on-site at POP could not open one, in many cases, due to negative ChexSystems reports. According to an analysis by Popular Community Bank conducted on the 175 participants who there was no record of an account being opened, 81 participants or 46% had ChexSystems profiles. Most of the negative ChexSystem profiles indicated some prior misuse of an account, e.g., owing a balance on a previous account. Over 60% of the negative balances owed on previous accounts were less than $500, but the range owed varied from $38 to $6,423. Only 33 profiles in ChexSystem reported fraudulent activity on a previous account.

FINANCIAL COUNSELING

As part of the field experiment, about one-half of the POP employees were offered the opportunity to attend one-on-one financial counseling during their prescribed work hours. The counseling was provided by New York City's Financial Empowerment Centers, which were established in 2008 and offer financial counseling at over 20 locations citywide to all New York City residents at no cost to participants. Center counselors are trained to help clients on a range of financial issues, such as money management, budgeting, selecting safe and affordable financial products, and credit and debt management. For the purposes of this pilot, counselors were informed of the unique needs of this client group with reference to direct deposit and the Popular accounts. For example, counseling might address transitioning from the use of alternative financial services, how to address and negotiate problems with prior banks, or the maintenance of accounts and direct deposit should clients' employment situations change. However, the counselors also engaged with each client in a full financial health assessment that looked at their finances overall and helped them to establish a plan of action for addressing a range of needs such as: budgeting for transitions, credit review and repair, reducing debt and planning for future needs. Sessions lasted between 30 minutes to an hour, and participants offered counseling were credited a full day of work with pay to attend their initial session. Participants also had the option to return for a second session on work time. Additional sessions may also have been compensated at the counselor's recommendation.

At the POP professional development day, the POP specialists introduced financial counseling and facilitated the scheduling of appointments for those participants who signed up for counseling. The financial counseling treatment in this study was not offered to every participant, but was randomized by month of hire and by borough in which the POP site was located. The study did not use individual random assignment for several reasons, including logistical complexity as well as concerns that co-workers would communicate about what they learned in counseling and bias the comparisons. During the first half of the study period, POP sites in two of the four boroughs were randomly assigned to offer financial counseling to participants. Because treatment effects may be correlated with differences between sites, the counseling assignment was switched after approximately half the participants were recruited. At this point, the sites that did not previously offer counseling became the sites offering counseling as shown in Table 1. This permits an analysis of site-specific effects, as well as "treatment" effects, in isolation.

TABLE 1. FINANCIAL EDUCATION CENTER COUNSELING OFFER TREATMENT ASSIGNMENT

	Recruitment Period	
Borough	January-February 2012	March-May 2012
Bronx	FEC offer	No FEC offer
Brooklyn	FEC offer	No FEC offer
Manhattan	No FEC offer	FEC offer
Queens	No FEC offer	FEC offer

According to administrative data, approximately 186 (37%) participants who were offered counseling actually attended counseling at a Financial Empowerment Center, as well as just two participants in the comparison group. Just over half of participants (53%) attended just one counseling session, 32% attended two or three sessions, and the remaining 15% attended between four and 13 sessions. Table 2 shows the number of clients in the counseling (or treatment) group and the comparison (or control) group by counseling attendance. The average effects of counseling across the counseling group are diffused by the nearly two-thirds of clients (63%) who do not take part. Because the choice to seek counseling is nonrandom and correlated financial outcomes in ways that would bias the results, we instead use counseling group membership to predict take up of counseling using a two-stage least square instrumental variable approach (2SLS-IV). This permits presentation of average "intent to treat" as well as estimated "treatment on treated" effects related to being offered counseling and actually receiving counseling.[7]

TABLE 2. TAKE UP OF COUNSELING AT NYC FINANCIAL EMPOWERMENT CENTERS

	Counseling Group	Comparison	Total
Attended FEC	186	2	188
No Counseling	319	527	846
Total	505	529	1034

The unbiased effects of counseling can be estimated using this research design, but the effects of account access cannot be estimated in a similar way. Accounts were offered universally to all POP employees and there was no variation in access to accounts or the promotion of accounts by site or time period. There is not a way to identify the effects of account access that can overcome the biases inherent in which clients selected to open and use accounts.

---

[7] This estimate is more precisely the Local Average Treatment Effect (LATE). It represents the effects among clients who were most likely to be induced into counseling by assignment based on the random nature of POP location and month of starting in POP. It is valid as long as people did not seek out POP services and locations because of some prior knowledge of the offer of counseling--which seems highly plausible. It is not the same estimate we might predict if all clients participated in counseling, nor the effect just among clients most interested in counseling. Rather, it is the estimated effects of for the marginal client induced into counseling by assignment (hence the "local" label).

Data

The data for this study consists of a combination of self-reported and administrative data collected at baseline and six and 12 months from enrollment in the study. Six months post-enrollment is a critical juncture as it coincides with the end of participants' enrollment in POP and for two thirds of participants it marks their entry into unemployment. The number of records from each data source is summarized in Table 3. The Parks Department provided administrative data on program participation, demographic characteristics and post-program employment data, and OFE provided administrative data on counseling attendance. In addition, a baseline survey assessing current banking status and financial situation, behaviors, and attitudes as well as collecting demographic characteristics was administered on-site during study recruitment. Approximately 1,300 POP participants between January and May 2012 were recruited, and 1,034 participants consented to participate. These clients also received a $25 gift card to compensate them for their time involved in data collection. A follow-up survey was administered at all POP sites six months following enrollment at POP exit seminars, as the six-month data collection coincided with the end of participants' employment with POP. Participants not attending the exit seminar were sent the survey by mail. Approximately 39% of the six-month surveys were administered on-site, with the remaining 61% administered through the mail, and the combined response rate for all six-month surveys was 58%. All 12-month follow up surveys were all completed via the mail and the response rate was 48%. Mailed 12-month surveys used a three-wave design with two reminder postcards, $10 pre-incentives and $10 metro card post-incentives. Because participants were recruited on a rolling basis and the last client was recruited in early May 2012, follow-up data collection took place through July 2013.

Data regarding debt levels, delinquencies, and credit utilization rates were collected at intake and then at six and 12 months after enrollment using extracts from printed credit reports. Credit reports were accessed through TransUnion, read into a machine readable format and then matched to the baseline participant survey data using a combination of date of birth and the last four digits in the participant's Social Security number.[8]

Credit report records used in this project contain data on outstanding debt, payment history and status, available credit, as well as public record information such as bankruptcy filings and tax liens. These reports represent a snapshot of credit at a point in time, but also contain historic information on negative items such as delinquency and bankruptcy. Credit reports are unavailable for about 15% of study participants at baseline. The rate of missing reports overall declines over the study (see Appendix A-4), but only 80% of participants have credit report data in all periods examined. In addition, just over half (55%) of study participants do not have a credit score reported. Even among those with a credit report available, as many as 40% do not have a credit score reported from

---

[8] The reports were conducted as "soft pulls" and were not recorded as an inquiry that could harm credit history.

TransUnion. This is largely due to people having little formal credit activity or having few active accounts.

For participants who opened a Popular checking account and signed a data release form, Popular provide data on monthly account balances and fees from January 2012 through June 2013. Bank account data is available for approximately 32% of study participants, a relatively low rate relative to the 49% of clients who applied to open accounts with Popular Community Bank. The lack of data is due to several factors: the number of POP participants who were unable to open accounts as previously reported but also the inability to match records due to missing data fields.

TABLE 3. SAMPLE SIZE BY DATA SOURCE

	Baseline	6-Month	12-Month
Credit Report	884	9?8	997
Credit Score	415	4?9	449
Survey	1034	5?9	499
Bank Record		334	

Table 4 summarizes selected aspects of the overall study population and then the counseling and comparison groups. Baseline data on the POP participants enrolled in the study paint a portrait of a very financially vulnerable population from traditionally disadvantaged communities, as would be expected for a population transitioning off of public benefits. Most are single women with children, and one-in-five live in a homeless shelter. Approximately one-third report having a bank account in the month prior to enrolling in POP, and 74% report using alternative financial services, including money orders and check cashers. The average credit score of 558 is well below what lenders would consider a good credit score, although as stated above, almost half of the participants with a credit report did not have enough credit history or activity to have a credit score.

TABLE 4: BASELINE CHARACTERISTICS OF STUDY PARTICIPANTS

	Total	Counseling Group	Comparison Group
Attended FEC	18.2%	36.8%	0.4%
Male	22%	27	16%
Age	35.5	35.	35.4
Married	8.5%	8.3	8.7%
Have Children	76%	73	79%
Public Housing/Staying with Friends	24%	25	23%
Homeless	20%	19	21%
Banked	34%	33	35%
Use Alternative Financial Services	74%	72	75%
Self-Reported Financial Literacy (5pt)	3.3	3.3	3.4
In Control of Finances (5pt)	2.8	2.8	2.8
Savings ($)	122	88	156
Debt (excluding mortgage) ($)	5,316	4,817	5,901
Credit Score	558	561	555

Looking at the characteristics of the participants by treatment group, the counseling group and the comparison group are comparable on some variables, such as age, marital status, living in public housing, being banked and self-reported financial literacy and attitudes. Other items, such as gender, savings and debt levels, appear skewed such that the comparison group appears to have more savings and debt (and perhaps more financial activity in general). These differences do not hold up to common statistical tests, but do suggest that including control variables in estimated effects would be appropriate.

Table 5 summarizes these same variables based on which participants are included in each data sources. The last line shows the total number of participants in each form of data (also shown as percent missing in Appendix A-4). One concern with high rates of missing data is the potential of non-response bias. This table shows that that selected aspects of the overall study population are comparable in most respects. The 12-month follow up was (predictably) less likely to be reported by people who indicate they are homeless. Surprisingly, given the magnitude of missing data, none of these other factors are statistically different.

TABLE 5. BASELINE CHARACTERISTICS BY SUBPOPULATION WITH EACH DATA SOURCE

	Total	Credit Report*	Credit Score*	6-Month Survey	12-Month Survey	Bank Data
Counseling Group	48.8%	49.4%	44.6%	45.7%	48.5%	45.8%
Attended Counseling	18.2%	18.3%	19%	17.5%	18.6%	17.4%
Male	22%	22%	17%	22%	25%	15%
Age	35.5	35.6	35.7	37.5	38.5	34.2
Married	8.5%	8.5%	9.8%	7.2%	8.0%	8.4%
Have Children	76%	76%	76%	73%	70%	81%
Public Housing/Staying w/ Friends	24%	24%	23%	24%	25%	25%
Homeless	20%	20%	16%	15%	12%	20%
Banked	34%	34%	45%	37%	37%	28%
Use Alternative Financial Services	74%	73%	75%	73%	77%	76%
In Control of Finances (5pt)	3.3	3.3	3.3	3.3	3.3	3.3
Self-Reported Fin. Literacy (5pt)	2.8	2.8	2.7	2.7	2.8	2.7
Savings ($)	122	119	105	87	124	81
Debt (excluding mortgage) ($)	5,316	5,316	9,761	6,496	5,977	4,960
Credit Score	558	558	558	562	562	555
OBSERVATIONS	1,034	879	415	599	499	334

* = baseline data

The final aspect of the data worth noting is that all POP employees seem to be on a positive financial trajectory in terms of improving credit scores, being banked and reduced use of alternative financial institutions (See Table 6). The most dramatic change over the study period is the percent of participants who report being banked, moving from one-third at baseline to almost 60% at six months and still over half at 12 months. Table 6 also demonstrates the key purpose of the POP program: employment. POP is a transitional employment program for people coming off of public assistance with the goal of moving people into unsubsidized employment. The six-month survey was collected just as employment through POP was ending (and for many at their actual exit seminar from the program), and only 18% reported having found other employment at that time. About one-third report being employed at 12 months, six months after exiting the POP program.[9] This self-reported employment rate is in line with POP's overall statistics of two-thirds of participants entering unemployment after the program. It is also a reasonably high rate relative to other transitional jobs programs,[10] especially given the extremely poor job market between 2010 and 2012 for low-wage workers. Nevertheless, it is critical to keep the context of unemployment in mind in this study. Populations who lack employment and face extreme levels of financial instability may still benefit from financial counseling and access to mainstream financial products and services, but expectations about the degree to which these services can resolve larger issues need to be held in check.[11]

TABLE 6. CHANGES IN POP POPULATION OVER THE 12-MONTH STUDY

	Baseline	6 Months	12 Months
Credit Score	558	561	570
Banked	34%	59%	54%
Uses alternative finance	74%	70%	64%
Employed full time	100%	5.9%	12.1%
Employed part time	0%	11.5%	23.1%

Analysis and Results

This analysis uses a POP employee's "assignment" (defined here simply as when and where they worked in POP) to the counseling group as a random event that can be then used to predict take-up of financial counseling. This provides a valid instrument to identify counseling and estimate unbiased impacts of actually attending a financial counseling session. This is sometimes called an adjusted or estimated treatment-on-treated (TOT) impact. Other approaches proved less effective. Our estimates of overall average effects of assignment to (intent to treat, or ITT) were swamped by the two-thirds of POP participants who were offered counseling but declined to take up services. Our estimates of just those clients who took part in counseling were biased since these clients were

---

[9] Through the Parks Department, we were able to collect additional hourly wage data on 244 participants who found employment outside of POP. The average hourly wage was $11.10 with a maximum of $28.90, and the average number of days worked during the study period was 229 days. When a control for income earned outside of POP was included in the analysis, there was no significant difference in the estimated treatment effects.

[10] See: Gretchen Kirby, Heather Hill, LaDonnaPavetti and Jon Jacobson. (2002). "Transitional Jobs: Stepping Stones to Unsubsidized Employment." Mathmatica Policy Research.
http://www.mathematica-mpr.com/PDFs/transitionalreport.pdf

[11] We do not find statistical differences in the likelihood of finding work outside of POP between those who have and have not attended financial counseling, nor assignment to sites where/when counseling is offered.

motivated to attend counseling sessions due to their particular financial situation (e.g., those most in crisis attended).

All analysis shown in this report is regression adjusted, ordinary least squares (OLS) or instrumental variable 2-stage least squares (2SLS) or 2-stage probit/tobit specifications (only for dichotomous dependent variables and those with non-normal distributions). Results displayed here only include the estimated coefficients on the counseling variable (estimated coefficients for control variables are available upon request).

Estimates of being assigned to financial counseling (or ITT) are labeled "counseling group". This is the best estimate of the average effects *of making counseling available* at the POP sites *regardless of take-up*. The impact of actually receiving financial counseling (TOT) is labeled as "Attended FEC." This is estimated using an instrumental variable (or IV) to provide an estimate of effects for people induced into attending counseling, providing an unbiased estimate of the impact of clients *being offered and attending financial counseling*.[12]

Each regression estimate measures the average change in the outcome of interest controlling for the initial value of that outcome (where possible) and limited set of baseline controls variables. Control variables include (baseline) client age, gender, marital status, ever having a bank account, and use of alternative financial products (such as payday loans). In all cases, the standard errors are clustered at the POP site by treatment group level (14 clusters) since employees and neighborhoods at a particular POP site are likely correlated. Tables show results separately for the full 12-month period (left column), the first six-month period (center column), and the second six-month period (right column). Statistically significant effects are marked with asterisks.[13]

CREDIT OUTCOMES

TABLE 7. CAUSAL ESTIMATES OF COUNSELING ON CREDIT SCORES

Credit Score	0 to 12 months	0 to 6 months	6 to 12 months
Counseling Group (ITT)	0.206	6.363	-4.805
	(0.965)	(0.151)	(0.170)
Attended FEC (TOT)	0.454	14.49	-10.91
	(0.962)	(0.113)	(0.091)
Observations	343	375	404

Beginning with credit scores, Table 7 shows some increase in scores for clients who took part in counseling at six months, but not at standard levels of significance. At 12 months this result reversed, mostly the result of the control groups catching up to the progress the treatment groups made in the first six months. Both the ITT and TOT estimates are positive, with the estimated effects

---

[12] An alternative is a Bloom Estimator, which divides the ITT estimates by the participation rate, as an estimate of the effect size if participation had been complete.

[13] In the tables that follow: * = 0.05 significance level, ** = 0.01 significance level, *** = .001 significance level.

of attending counseling about three times the level of the overall average effect (recall about 1/3 of POP participants took part in counseling, consistent with Bloom estimator results). However, only 343 study participants had credit scores reported in all three periods, reducing the statistical power of these estimates. None of these findings meets standard statistical benchmarks for significance.

TABLE 8. CAUSAL ESTIMATES OF COUNSELING ON THE PERCENTAGE OF DEBT THAT IS PAST DUE

Pct Past Due	0 to 12 months	0 to 6 months	6 to 12 months
Counseling Group (ITT)	-0.0518**	-0.0183	-0.0318*
	(0.004)	(0.340)	(0.041)
Attended FEC (TOT)	-0.140**	-0.0494	-0.0878*
	(0.002)	(0.305)	(0.030)
Observations	879	879	995

The estimates in Table 8 on percentage of debt past due uses the larger sample of clients with credit reports (n=879 for all three periods). These estimates indicate that, on average, offering counseling produces a 5% reduction in falling behind on debt payments over 12 months, and 14% for those attending counseling. Because this outcome is constrained to 0% to 100%, we worry this finding could be a result of the distribution of this variable. However, the results are robust to alternative specifications such as a Tobit model. The results at six months are directionally appropriate, but not statistically significant. The results overall show a consistent pattern of financial counseling, helping individuals stay current with their debt payments, at least measured by the percentage of debt that is past due. Figure 3 further displays these estimates as a line graph, including dashed lines for the confidence intervals of the results.

FIGURE 3: INTENT TO TREAT PERCENTAGE PAST DUE

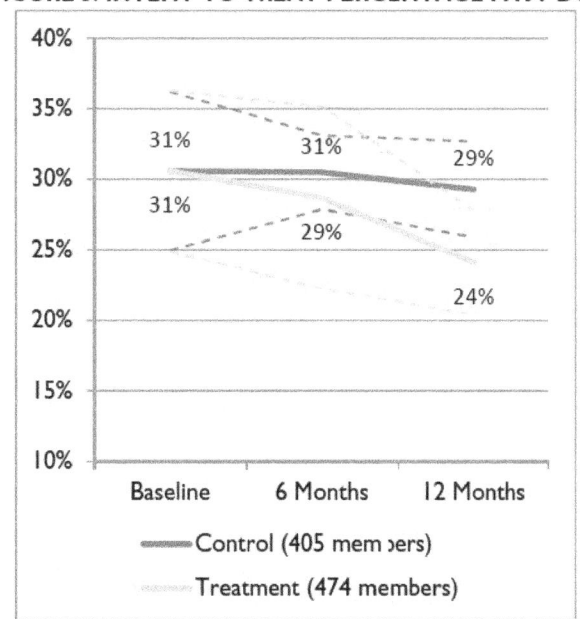

Past due debt is an important determinant of credit score. Therefore, it may be surprising to see significant reduction in the percentage past due debt without similar movement in the credit scores. This apparent discrepancy stems from the different samples available for the two outcomes. Less than half of this population has sufficient credit history on file to receive a credit score. As shown below in Table 9, there are no significant reductions in the percentage of debt past due among the people who do have credit scores. The reductions in debt past due are concentrated in the people without credit scores (without scores as of at least one endpoint necessary to calculate the change). Large changes in percentage past due are also dominated by people who had zero debt at one endpoint and positive, but completely past due debt at the other (e.g. went from 0% past due to 100%, or vice versa).

TABLE 9. CAUSAL ESTIMATES OF COUNSELING ON THE PERCENTAGE OF DEBT THAT IS PAST DUE BY CREDIT SCORE REPORTING

Pct Past Due	0 to 12 months	0 to 6 months	6 to 12 months
	With Score Reported		
Attended FEC (TOT)	-0.0359	-0.0493	-0.00379
	(0.433)	(0.381)	(0.895)
Observations	343	375	404
	Without Score Reported		
Attended FEC (TOT)	-0.193**	-0.0426	-0.126*
	(0.006)	(0.411)	(0.016)
Observations	536	504	591

BANKING OUTCOMES

One objective of the design of counseling and the offer of a bank account in this study was to understand how counselors might aid clients in better managing banking services and products. As shown in Table 6 above, POP participants showed a dramatic increase in reporting a bank account. One potential outcome of counseling would be that counseling clients are more likely to report having a bank account in follow-up surveys.

TABLE 10. CAUSAL ESTIMATES OF COUNSELING ON BANKING STATUS

Banked	0 to 12 months	0 to 6 months	6 to 12 months
Counseling Group (ITT)	-0.0002	-0.0370	0.0358
	(0.996)	(0.166)	(0.191)
Attended FEC (TOT)	0.0004	-0.0948	0.0973
	(0.997)	(0.214)	(0.218)
Observations	495	593	362

Note: marginal effects.

Table 10 shows estimated rates of reporting being banked (that is having an active checking or savings account) using a Probit 2-stage IV model. Although POP participation in general is associated with a large increase in being banked, there is no differential increase in being banked related to financial counseling. Counseling is associated with a positive increase in bank accounts in the 6-12 month period (likely due to the persistence of accounts open while employed by POP), but the estimates are not significant statistically. Figure 4 shows these results graphically: the increase in the average rate of reporting being banked increased starkly for all POP participants. Effects again here may not be significant due to the smaller number of respondents who completed the follow-up surveys.

FIGURE 4: AVERAGE RATE OF REPORTING BEING BANKED

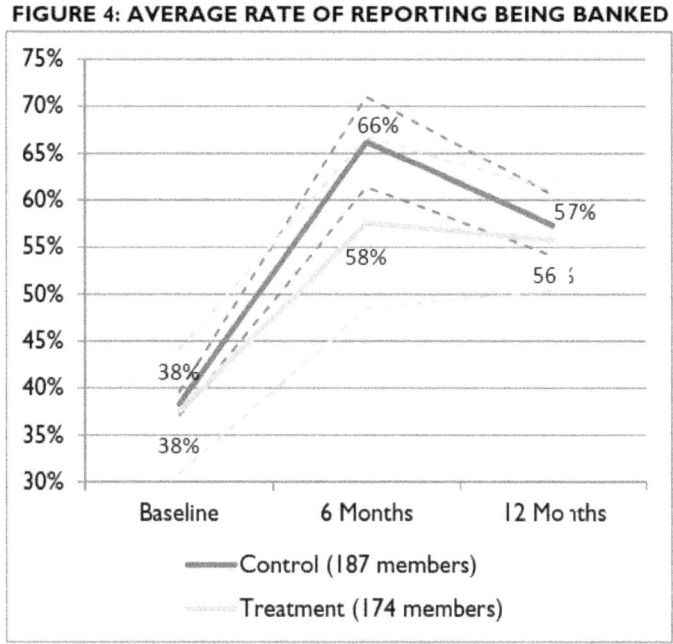

Monthly statements provided by Popular Community Bank, although only available for a subset of POP participants, offer more detail in how those people who have accounts are using them during and after taking part in POP. This analysis provides an indication of how study participants are using their bank accounts. Not every client had a full year of account statements (clients may have delayed opening accounts or closed them). On average, we observe 7.7 bank statements per study participant for whom bank data was able to be matched, and only 78 of the 334 participants for which we had account data still had open accounts as of June 2013.[14]

Account balances in this analysis are measured in log dollars (we use the log of balance because the distributions are highly skewed with many near zero and a few very large values). The balance is also calculated as the average of the within-month average balance recorded in each monthly statement. Any negative values are recorded as zero. It should be noted that it is unclear what the "correct" outcome for participants might be. Carrying a larger bank balance is often attributed to sound financial management, but if a client pays down high cost debt, lower balances may be just as sound of a financial decision.

---

[14] Although not shown, we did test for the effects of counseling on account opening and termination. We do not find evidence that counseling significantly increased the rate of opening accounts or the amount of time the bank accounts are open.

TABLE 11. CAUSAL ESTIMATES OF COUNSELING ON AVERAGE BALANCE

Average Balance	Full Study Period	0 to 6 months	6 months to End
Counseling Group (ITT)	0.117	0.118	-0.447
	(0.642)	(0.678)	(0.063)
Attended FEC (TOT)	0.316	0.318	-1.115
	(0.609)	(0.650)	(0.053)
Observations	334	334	216

Table 11 shows the effects of financial counseling on log average balances. There are no statistically significant differences, but there is directional evidence that counseling actually reduces bank balances in the 6-12 month period (post POP). Looking at the actual (non-log) balances this translates into about a $41 decrease in average balance for counseled clients. There does not appear to be a relationship between an individual paying down debt and bank balances based on further analyses, however.

The average person in the bank data has an account balance of $107 during the first 6 months of the study, and $91 in 6-12 month period (post POP). About 28% of the POP participants in the bank data paid at least one bank fee: typically insufficient funds or returned item fees. On average, fees were about $47 over the lifetime of the account. Counseling could potentially help clients to avoid such fees, and Table 12 shows the effects of counseling on average fees.

TABLE 12. CAUSAL ESTIMATES OF COUNSELING ON AVERAGE BANK FEES

Account Fees	0 to 12 months	0 to 6 months	6 to 12 months
Counseling Group (ITT)	0.400	0.379	0.364
	(0.243)	(0.269)	(0.126)
Attended FEC (TOT)	1.079	1.023	0.908
	(0.246)	(0.274)	(0.112)
Observations	334	334	216

The results in Table 12 are not statistically significant, but suggestive that counseling may actually increase fees incurred for insufficient funds and returned items. One potential explanation for this counterintuitive result is counselors could promote the use of automatic electronic funds transfers for bill payments.

FINANCIAL PLANNING OUTCOMES

Six survey questions related to taking steps to managing personal finances "in the last six months." Items in this index include (1) reviewing a credit report, (2) creating a debt payment plan, (3) establishing a new source of credit, (4) using a savings program, (5) increasing amounts put into savings, and (6) increasing amounts put into paying off debt. These questions could capture people who intend to make forward-looking changes in their financial behavior.

TABLE 13. CAUSAL ESTIMATES OF COUNSELING ON FINANCIAL PLANNING

Financial Plan Index	0 to 12 months	0 to 6 months	6 to 12 months
Counseling Group (ITT)	0.0298	0.0970*	-0.0842
	(0.563)	(0.040)	(0.187)
Attended FEC (TOT)	0.0817	0.256**	-0.231
	(0.548)	(0.006)	(0.124)
Observations	494	590	354

Table 13 shows that counseling is associated with positive changes for the zero to six month period. Additional analysis into the components of the index suggest this is largely driven by reviewing a credit report. Most survey respondents did not report reviewing a report in the prior six months at baseline. Credit reports were commonly used as part of counseling sessions, and we might expect employees in POP to also be seeking credit while employed and therefore motivated to monitor their credit reports. Creating a 5-item index excluding reviewing a credit report question results in much smaller, less statistically significant effects.

The questions in this index ask about steps taken over the past six months. Some steps, such as signing up for a savings program or creating a debt repayment plan, may only need to be taken once, assuming the participant sticks with them. The 6-12 month results primarily capture the fact that the credit report review that is part of the counseling session but not repeated after counseling is completed and the client exits POP. Further analysis of the relationship between paying down debt and this index do not reveal any insights into causal pathways—that is, we cannot isolate financial planning, or even checking a credit report specifically, as contributing directly to how counseling clients are reducing the percentage of debt past due.

SUMMARY OF FINDINGS

Financial counseling is associated with:

- A decrease in the percentage of debt that is past due for both six and 12 month periods. The estimated effect is quite large and seems to be concentrated in people who do not have credit scores and borrow less than the typical person in this population. In particular, the effect is driven by the 10% of the sample who experienced the maximum change in this metric (+/- 100%).
- An increase in credit scores at the six month mark, which coincided with the end of employment through POP and a return to unemployment for most participants, but no measurable effect by the 12 month follow-up credit report. Scores are only available for a subset of study participants, however.
- An increase in financial planning behaviors, especially reviewing a credit report, but only at the six month point of the study.
- A decrease in account balances held and an increase in bank fees, although neither estimate is significant.

Below is a summary table showing the average the effects of financial counseling over the full study period and the first six months. Each is shown as effect sizes or standard deviation units (sigma units).

TABLE 14. SUMMARY OF ESTIMATES OF THE EFFECTS OF COUNSELING

Outcome	Expected Direction	12-Month TOT		6-Month TOT	
		Effect (sigma units)	Significance	Effect (sigma units)	Significance
Credit Score	+	0.01		0.24	
Percent of Debt Past Due	-	-0.32	**	-0.11	
Balance in Collections	-	-0.18		-0.15	
Revolving Credit Available	+	-0.04		0.00	
Banked	+	0.00		-0.20	
Savings frequency	+	-0.04		-0.07	
Emergency savings	+	0.18		-0.20	
Have a financial goal	+	-0.03		0.26	
Financial worry	-	-0.26		-0.04	
AltFinance Index	-	0.18		0.45	
Planning Index	+	0.12		0.38	**
Confidence Index	+	-0.25		-0.10	
Popular Community Bank Average Balance	+	0.14		0.15	
Popular Community Bank Ending Balance	+	-0.16		0.06	
Popular Community Bank Fees	-	0.51		0.48	
Popular Community Bank Number of Statements	+	0.15		NA	

Insights from Implementation

The lessons learned from implementation of the AFCO pilot may be of interest to other programs interested in integrating financial access and counseling into their existing services, but the findings from the qualitative research conducted with program stakeholders and participants also offers insights into the findings of the study. Through a series of one-hour interviews conducted with program stakeholders including POP participants,[15] POP staff, financial counselors and Popular

---

[15] CFED conducted in-depth in person interviews with 11 POP participants who enrolled in the study, who had varying levels of participation with the banking access and financial counseling aspects of the pilot. CFED offered participants a $50 incentive for participating in the interview, which each lasted an hour and were held on-site at a Parks Department location.

Bank staff, we documented the strengths and weaknesses of the pilot's implementation and the experiences of the participants in three key areas: account-take up, account use and financial counseling take-up.

ACCOUNT TAKE-UP

The rate of participants being banked jumped from approximately one-third the month prior to enrolling in AFCO to 59% at six months and still 55% a year later. Just over half of participants in the study applied to open an account with Popular Community Bank, which suggests that there was an unmet demand for safe, affordable financial products among this population. However, the Parks Department had worked with OFE and financial institutions to offer similar products in the past without the same level of take-up, which also suggests that elements of the pilot's design and implementation were a factor. Key elements were:

- *The timing of the offer and convenience of the account opening*: The offer of the account was embedded into the POP orientation day and repeated again at the first professional development date several weeks later. It was not treated as an optional component of the schedule, but was built into the orientation that all participants went through. Bank representatives were also on-site to open accounts so that participants did not have to visit a branch after work to complete the process. However, one downside of the on-site account opening was that the ChexSystems verification could not be conducted on site, which caused a delay in people being informed that their account could not be opened if there was a ChexSystems report.
- *Messaging of the banking offer:* The account offer was delivered by the POP specialists, who were former POP participants. The specialists used real-life examples to talk about the benefits of bank accounts and direct deposit. Participants interviewed expressed appreciation for the specialists' experience with POP and their down-to-earth demeanor in presentations. Peer-to-peer education and support was critical in making these products relevant to POP participants, and that approach was coupled with the expert information that the bankers on-site could provide when participants had questions about banking and the accounts.
- *Providing incentives*: Participants were offered a $25 incentive if they enrolled in direct deposit, and several participants cited wanting to take advantage of that offer as a reason they decided to open an account with Popular.

ACCOUNT USE AND MAINTENANCE

While the demand for the accounts was high, the account data from Popular suggest that not all participants used their accounts successfully. Accounts were open for an average of eight months, and the data demonstrated that the accounts could be relatively expensive for those that incurred fees on the account. Only 28% of accounts generated fees, but for those that did, the average fees charged were approximately 50% of the average balance they carried over the life of the account. Of the 334 accounts opened through the pilot, 23% were still open as of June 2013.[16]

The interviews with participants shed some light on the issues with account use. While participants found the Popular account features appealing, it seems that not all understood the fee structure of the account. They remembered the account being "free" and so were confused when fees for various transactions such as use of out-of-network ATMs were taken out of the account. One participant reported that she closed her Popular account because of the fees she was charged. Another theme that came up several times in the interviews was the link between bank accounts and employment. One participant put it simply, "I can't use a bank if I'm not working." Knowing that as many as two-thirds of POP participants were unemployed after POP, the number of closed accounts is perhaps not surprising.

However, the fact that many the Popular bank accounts were closed does not necessarily mean that the participants were unbanked at the end of the study. According to the participant surveys, the number of participants banked fell between six and 12 months after enrollment, but only by four percentage points. Participants may have stopped using their Popular accounts and instead used or opened accounts with other financial institutions. The interviews revealed that some participants' impressions of and experiences with Popular Community Bank were mixed. Popular did not have a high profile with many participants. Some people had not heard of the bank or were not aware of the bank's locations, branches or ATMs (possibly contributing to the fees incurred by some), even though information on locations and the ATM network was provided during the orientation. There was a general impression among participants that Popular wasn't a convenient bank, and some, both in interviews and at POP presentations, expressed a strong preference to bank with financial institutions that had a larger presence in the New York City market. Popular Community Bank's reputation in the community may have played a role in whether or not participants maintained the banking relationship after the pilot.

COUNSELING TAKE-UP

POP participants were offered a full eight hours of paid work time to attend financial counseling and could access one-on-one counseling with a trained counselor at no charge. Nevertheless, only 37% of people offered financial counseling attended counseling. After examining the programmatic data from implementation, it appears that the first major challenge in getting participants into counseling was scheduling appointments. When the pilot was launched, the POP specialists asked

---

[16] This level of account retention was considered good by Popular Community Bank. It is lower than account retention rates reported for other account access programs, such as local Bank On programs. Bank On Savannah and Louisville have reported account retention rates of 86% and 85% after one and two years, respectively. However, the population participating in Bank On in these communities chose to open accounts voluntarily rather than as a part of a research pilot and is likely not as highly financially vulnerable or unemployed as the POP population.

each participant who expressed interest in counseling to provide contact information so that they could follow up to schedule the financial counseling appointment. However, the specialists were not able to contact the majority of those that signed up after only a few weeks. Multiple attempts were made to reach each participant by phone and email, or in person in some cases, but many POP participants proved unreachable and didn't receive a counseling appointment. This issue speaks to the transient nature of this population, one in five of whom was homeless at baseline. For those that did schedule an appointment, the attendance rate was 65%, on par with attendance rates for other similar groups, according to several financial counselors. In addition, the offer to attend counseling was only made once by the specialists, as opposed to the offer of bank accounts, which was offered on two separate occasions. Repetition of the offer, combined with the right messaging about the benefits of counseling, may have helped increase the take-up.

The financial counselors interviewed pointed out that repeated counseling sessions, a minimum of two or three, are usually necessary in order for financial counseling to have a substantial effect on someone's personal finances. The attendance data from the Financial Empowerment Centers showed that 53% of participants attended just one counseling session, 22% attended two, and only 25% attended three or more sessions. Had the program placed greater emphasis on encouraging POP participants to attend multiple financial counseling sessions, we may have seen a greater effect of counseling on the outcomes of interest in the study.[17]

Insights for Practice and Policy

The leadership at POP and OFE carefully designed a program with high fidelity and attention to details related to communication and timing of the offer of accounts and counseling. The data show promising signs that the offer of counseling is related to a decrease in past due debt, with credit scores and measures of financial planning also directionally positive.

However, the level of financial vulnerability in this population suggests that the findings from this study may not be generalizable to the overall adult population. The POP population faces additional barriers and challenges that may influence the impact of counseling on their financial capability, such as a lack of experience with mainstream financial products and high rates of unemployment. Despite these qualifications, the pilot can offer several important insights on the topic of expanded financial access that are instructive for both policy makers and program administrators.

---

[17] We tested the effect of attending multiple sessions on the small sample of those that attended counseling, and in general, more sessions, especially three or more sessions, do seem correlated with positive changes in credit score and banking status. These results are not causal in nature as showing up to (or asking for) more counseling sessions signals willingness or motivation to make financial changes.

Insight #1: Integrating Access to Financial Products and Services is Feasible at Scale

The AFCO pilot is a example of a public program successfully integrating the offer of appropriate financial products and services into an existing program for a high-need population. The Parks Opportunity Program is one of the largest transitional employment programs in the nation that offers participants an array of services—job training, computer skills, job search assistance and other workshops, and OFE and the Parks Department worked closely with partners to embed the account opening process and the offer of financial counseling into the existing program's structure, making the process as seamless as possible for the participants. The high take-up rate of the bank accounts suggests that unbanked participants had a strong desire to become banked and would take advantage of an opportunity if offered an account with agreeable terms that was easy to open.

The results from this study suggest that embedding financial product offers along with financial counseling within the context of public programs can be an effective way to promote financial access and financial capability. Partnerships between social and human services programs and financial institutions and financial counseling networks should be considered and encouraged.

Workforce programs in particular offer an ideal setting for these types of additional offerings as programs are working to increase the incomes of participants and move them into the labor force or unsubsidized employment. Counseling has the potential to help people plan and make effective choices about how to manage their income as well as manage their finances as they move into full time work. The bank account could also be a helpful tool to manage their earnings and expenses as they move from benefits into financial independence.

And while this pilot was focused on integrating access to financial products and counseling into a subsidized government employment program, it was also a pilot that integrated these services at the place of –and point of—employment. There is much from this model that has implications for private sector employers who could consider integrating similar access to financial product and education services into the hiring and orientation process and ancillary Employee Assistance Programs.

Insight #2: Successful Account Use and Management is Challenging

While account take up was high, the data on the use and maintenance of accounts was less positive. On average, the accounts were only open for just under eight months, and at the end of the study, one in four accounts opened during the pilot were still open. This suggests that the program design was successful in getting people into accounts, but encouraging successful account use still needs further examination. It may be the case that a traditional bank account, even one with flexible and affordable terms, does not fully meet the needs of this financially vulnerable population, particularly when they no longer have a source of steady income. When income is scarce, charges such as out-of-network ATM fees and insufficient funds fees can be just as problematic as courtesy overdraft fees. It may be beneficial to look at ways to further improve the structure of accounts specifically for low-income consumers or increase the functionality of existing public benefits transaction products, such as electronic benefit transfer (EBT) cards, to better ease the transition into mainstream financial products.

Another potential way to improve account use would be to change the sequencing of the services offered to participants. In the AFCO pilot design, the offer of bank accounts occurred first and was repeated a second time before financial counseling was offered to the treatment group. While the financial counselors were informed the POP participants were offered bank accounts as a part of the pilot, the counseling itself was not connected to the offer of financial access and occurred after participants had opened accounts. Perhaps account use would have been more successful if participants had received financial counseling prior to opening accounts rather than subsequently, although this program design may likely have resulted in lower take-up of accounts.

Insight #3: More Transparency and Consistency in Account History Reporting Systems May Expand Access

For this pilot, Popular Community Bank agreed to be flexible in its standards for opening accounts for people with trouble managing an account in the past. However, even with this increased flexibility, approximately one-third of POP participants who opted to open an account were still denied. Many participants were denied accounts due to negative reports in ChexSystems, and the frequency with which this occurred highlights the need to closely scrutinize the structural barriers to financial access that are associated with this system. Consumers lack information about ChexSystems and how to resolve issues. The financial industry lacks universal practices about what triggers a negative report to ChexSystems (including types of issues and dollar amounts), what information about the account is disclosed to the reporting agency, what constitutes as leniency for second chance accounts, and how consumers are notified when there are issues to be resolved. Financial access could potentially be expanded by increasing the transparency of ChexSystems and improving standards for what financial institutions report to both the reporting agencies and customers. Regulators may be able to also do more to ensure that financially vulnerable individuals, who are most at risk of being denied access to mainstream financial products, are aware of the system, know how to access and use reports, and understand how to rectify or dispute outstanding issues. Much like efforts have expanded consumer knowledge of, access to, and use of credit reports, a similar effort would be valuable related to account histories.

Insight #4: Integrating Financial Counseling Can Be Complex Within a Multi-Site Work Program

POP employees were offered a full eight hours of paid work time to attend financial counseling and could access one-on-one counseling with a trained counselor at no charge. Nevertheless, only 37% of people offered financial counseling attended counseling. While above we documented that challenges with the implementation of the counseling, i.e., scheduling appointments for this difficult to contact population, may account for much of the low take-up rate, it is worth noting that the provision of highly customized one-on-one counseling is not as easy to seamlessly integrate into an existing program. Participants were still required to take time off of work and travel to another location for their counseling appointment, and given the nature of this transitional employment program and the array of other services offered to participants, taking time for financial counseling meant not taking part in other potentially valuable activities. Past experiences with clients in New York City have also shown there may be many reasons why more people did not attend a counseling session, including not understanding what the counseling would entail, thinking that counseling is not for people like them, or believing that they did not have enough money to address any issues.

Insight #5: Expectations of Impact from Financial Capability Interventions with Vulnerable Populations Should Have Realistic Context

Integrating financial capability services into POP is an innovative program design. POP employees are working to transition off public assistance and into unsubsidized employment. Yet, the participants in this situation are still highly financially vulnerable. All are at or below the poverty level with little or no savings and many have relatively large debts and a history of falling behind on bills. About half had thin credit files or no credit score. As many as one in five were homeless or living in shelters during the program, and roughly two-thirds were unemployed twelve months after completing POP. Given the context of their lives, it is unrealistic that an hour of financial counseling could have an outsized effect on their overall financial well-being. Indeed it is encouraging to see that access to a limited amount of financial counseling was able to produce several outcomes that—while small—helped the population make inroads toward reducing their debt, improving their credit and building financial management skills. While counseling may be more likely to make a bigger impact on participants who have reliable income and some basic measure of financial stability, the potential importance of counseling for highly vulnerable populations should not be undervalued.

References

Agarwal, S., Chomsisengphet, S., & Do, C. (2011). *Beyond race and gender: Financial access to low and moderate income households.* Working Paper. Washington, DC: U.S. Office of the Comptroller of the Currency.

Baker, C., & Dylla, D. (2007). *Analyzing the relationship between account ownership and financial education.* Asset Building Program, New America Foundation.

Barr, M. S. (2004). *Banking the poor: Policies to bring low-income Americans into financial mainstream.* In Brookings Institution, Research Brief.

Barr, M. S., & Sherraden, M. W. (2005). Institutions and inclusion in saving policy. In N. Retsinas & E. Belsky (Eds.), *Building assets, building wealth: Creating wealth in low-income communities.* Washington, DC: Brookings Institution Press.

Bayer, P. J., Bernheim, B. D., & Scholz, J. K. (2008). The effects of financial education in the workplace: Evidence from a survey of employers. *Economic Inquiry, 47*(4), 605-624.

Bernheim, B. D., & Garrett, D. M. (2003). The effects of financial education in the workplace: Evidence from a survey of households. *Journal of Public Economics, 87*(7-8), 1487-1519.

Bertrand, M., Mullainathan, S., & Shafir, E. (2006). Behavioral economics and marketing in aid of decision making among the poor. *Journal of Public Policy and Marketing, 25*(1), 8-23.

Beverly, S. G., McBride, A. M., & Schreiner, M. (2003). A framework of asset-accumulation stages and strategies. *Journal of Family and Economic Issues, 24*(2), 143-156.

Beverly, S., Sherraden, M., Cramer, R., Williams Shanks, T. R., Nam, Y., & Zhan, M. (2008). Determinants of asset holdings. In S. M. McKernan & M. W. Sherraden (Eds.), *Asset building and low-income families, part 4.* Washington, DC: Urban Institute Press.

Collins, J. M., & O'Rourke, C. M. (2010). Financial education and counseling – Still holding promise. *Journal of Consumer Affairs, 44*(3), 483-498.

Elliehousen, G., Lundquist, E. C., & Staten, M. E. (2007). The impact of credit counseling on subsequent borrower behavior. *Journal of Consumer Affairs, 41*(1), 1-28.

Fine, J., Leimbach, L., & Jacob, K. (2006). *Distributing prepaid cards through worker centers: A gateway to asset building for low-income households.* Center for Financial Services Innovation, Research Brief.

O'Brien, R. (2006). I eligible to Save? Asset Limits and the Saving Behavior of Welfare Recipients. *Journal of Community Practice, 16*(2), 183-199.

——— (2012). "We don't do banks": Financial lives of families on public assistance. *Georgetown Journal on Poverty Law & Policy, 19*, 485-498.

Prescott, E. S., & Tatar, D. D. (1999). Means of payment, the unbanked and EFT '99. *Federal Reserve Bank of Richmond Economic Quarterly, 85*(4), 49-70.

Romich, J., Waithaka, E., & Gordon, S. (2010). A Tool for Getting By or Getting Ahead? Consumers' Views on Prepaid Cards. Center for Financial Services Innovation. University of Wisconsin, Madison, April 2010 Symposium – Family Financial Security.

Appendix A1: Summary Tables

Summary Means	Means Baseline			Means 6-Month			Means 12-Month			Counts		
	Total	Control	Treatment	Total	Control	Treatment	Total	Control	Treatment	Total	Control	Treatment
Could pay unexpected expense of $500 (5pt)	2.4	2.3	2.4	2.6	2.6	2.6	2.6	2.6	2.6	355	184	171
Trust banks (5pt)	2.8	2.8	2.7	2.4	2.4	2.4	2.6	2.7	2.5	359	187	172
In control of finances (5pt)	2.7	2.7	2.7	2.8	2.8	2.8	2.8	2.8	2.8	337	174	163
Self-assessed financial literacy (5pt)	3.4	3.4	3.3	3.3	3.3	3.2	3.2	3.3	3.2	358	186	172
Can pay bills on time (5pt)	3.8	3.8	3.9	3.3	3.3	3.4	3.3	3.3	3.4	338	178	160
Frequency of Saving (7pt)	3.5	3.6	3.4	3.8	3.8	3.9	3.4	3.5	3.3	329	175	154
Banked (y/n)	0.38	0.40	0.36	0.62	0.67	0.57	0.57	0.57	0.56	361	187	174
Uses alternative finance (y/n)	0.85	0.87	0.82	0.83	0.81	0.86	0.99	1.00	0.99	155	77	78
Credit Score	562	557	568	563	556	571	569	567	572	340	177	163
Percentage of Debt Past Due	0.31	0.30	0.31	0.29	0.30	0.29	0.27	0.29	0.25	879	405	474
Percentage of Accts. Past Due	0.37	0.37	0.37	0.36	0.37	0.34	0.32	0.35	0.30	879	405	474
Number of Accts. In Collections	1.9	2.0	1.8	1.9	2.0	1.8	1.9	2.0	1.8	879	405	474
Revolving Credit Available ($)	420	367	466	423	353	483	415	312	477	879	405	474
Debt (excluding mortgage, $)	5,328	5,907	4,836	5,455	5,685	5,261	5,586	5,932	5,293	876	402	474
Monthly Debt Payment ($)	119	92	143	121	93	145	120	91	145	879	405	474
Amount Past Due ($)	1,927	2,193	1,700	1,887	2,150	1,663	1,878	2,149	1,647	879	405	474
Number of Inquiries	1.5	1.6	1.4	1.6	1.7	1.5	1.8	1.9	1.8	879	405	474
Public Records	0.5	0.5	0.5	0.5	0.5	0.5	0.4	0.4	0.4	879	405	474
Negative Reports on Credit	1.5	1.8	1.3	1.5	1.8	1.2	1.3	1.6	1.1	879	405	474
Revolving Balance ($)	185	178	190	186	193	180	197	168	222	872	402	470
Limit on Revolving Balance ($)	5,236	3,857	7,029	5,282	3,771	7,246	5,473	3,928	7,481	92	52	40
Percent of Revolving Credit Available	72	65	82	71	64	80	73	68	81	86	49	37
Balance in Collections ($)	1,350	1,570	1,162	1,390	1,607	1,204	1,426	1,591	1,285	879	405	474
Balance on Mortgage ($)	392	131	614	385	120	610	-	-	-	876	402	474
Balance on Closed Accounts ($)	2,152	2,469	1,882	2,082	2,341	1,860	2,095	2,355	1,872	879	405	474
Balance on Installment Accounts ($)	2,904	3,186	2,662	3,142	3,126	3,156	3,235	3,329	3,154	873	403	470
Number of Student Loans	0.6	0.7	0.5	0.6	0.6	0.5	0.6	0.7	0.5	879	405	474
Balance on Student Loans ($)	2,717	2,957	2,512	2,886	2,883	2,889	3,018	3,229	2,838	879	405	474
Number of Revolving Accounts	1.4	1.8	1.1	1.4	1.8	1.1	1.4	1.7	1.1	879	405	474
Number of Installment Accounts	1.5	1.7	1.3	1.5	1.7	1.4	1.6	1.8	1.5	879	405	474
Number of Mortgages	0.0	0.0	0.0	0.0	0.0	0.0	0.0	0.0	0.0	879	405	474

Summary Means	Baseline			Means 6-Month			12-Month			Counts		
	Total	Control	Treatment	Total	Control	Treatment	Total	Control	Treatment	Total	Control	Treatment
Number of Open Accounts	0.5	0.5	0.5	0.4	0.4	0.4	0.3	0.3	0.3	879	405	474
Number of Auto Loans	0.0	0.0	0.0	0.0	0.0	0.0	0.0	0.0	0.0	879	405	474
Number of Credit Cards	0.3	0.4	0.2	0.3	0.4	0.2	0.3	0.3	0.2	879	405	474
Number of Lines of Credit	0.0	0.0	0.0	0.0	0.0	0.0	0.0	0.0	0.0	879	405	474
Number of Sales Contracts	0.0	0.0	0.0	0.0	0.0	0.0	0.0	0.0	0.0	879	405	474
Number of Secured Accounts	0.0	0.0	0.0	0.0	0.0	0.0	0.0	0.0	0.0	879	405	474
Number of Unsecured Accounts	0.0	0.0	0.0	0.0	0.0	0.0	0.0	0.0	0.0	879	405	474
Number of Bankruptcies	0.0	0.0	0.0	0.0	0.0	0.0	0.0	0.0	0.0	879	405	474
Tax Liens	361	409	320	366	433	308	360	418	293	879	405	474

	Standard Deviations								
	Baseline			6-Month			12-Month		
	Total	Control	Treatment	Total	Control	Treatment	Total	Control	Treatmen:
Could pay unexpected expense of $500 (5pt)	1.3	1.2	1.3	1.3	1.2	1.3	1.3	1.2	1.3
Trust banks (5pt)	1.1	1.1	1.0	1.1	1.1	1.0	1.1	1.1	1.0
In control of finances (5pt)	1.1	1.1	1.1	1.1	1.1	1.1	1.1	1.1	1.1
Self-assessed financial literacy (5pt)	1.0	1.0	1.0	1.0	1.0	1.0	1.0	1.0	1.0
Can pay bills on time (5pt)	1.0	1.1	0.9	1.0	1.1	0.9	1.0	1.1	0.9
Frequency of Saving (7pt)	2.3	2.3	2.4	2.3	2.3	2.4	2.3	2.3	2.4
Banked (y/n)	0.49	0.49	0.48	0.49	0.49	0.48	0.49	0.49	0.48
Uses alternative finance (y/n)	0.44	0.44	0.43	0.44	0.44	0.43	0.44	0.44	0.43
Credit Score	62	61	63	62	61	63	62	61	63
Percentage of Debt Past Due	0.43	0.43	0.44	0.43	0.43	0.44	0.43	0.43	0.44
Percentage of Accts. Past Due	0.42	0.41	0.42	0.42	0.41	0.42	0.42	0.41	0.42
Number of Accts. In Collections	2.2	2.2	2.3	2.2	2.2	2.3	2.2	2.2	2.3
Revolving Credit Available	2,304	1,703	2,715	2,304	1,703	2,715	2,304	1,703	2,715
Debt (excluding mortgage)	14,052	13,800	14,259	14,052	13,800	14,259	14,052	13,800	14,259
Monthly Debt Payment	775	573	913	775	573	913	775	573	913
Amount Past Due	6,920	7,034	6,820	6,920	7,034	6,820	6,920	7,034	6,820
Number of Inquiries	1.9	1.8	1.9	1.9	1.8	1.9	1.9	1.8	1.9
Public Records	1.0	1.0	0.9	1.0	1.0	0.9	1.0	1.0	0.9
Negative Reports on Credit	2.5	3.0	2.0	2.5	3.0	2.0	2.5	3.0	2.0
Revolving Balance	1,454	1,006	1,750	1,454	1,006	1,750	1,454	1,006	1,750
Limit on Revolving Balance	7,935	4,726	10,577	7,935	4,726	10,577	7,935	4,726	10,577
Percent of Revolving Credit Available	36	40	27	36	40	27	36	40	27
Balance in Collections	2,862	3,301	2,413	2,862	3,301	2,413	2,862	3,301	2,413
Balance on Mortgage	9,990	2,628	13,366	9,990	2,628	13,366	9,990	2,628	13,366

| | Standard Deviations | | | | | | | | |
| | Baseline | | | 6-Month | | | 12-Month | | |
	Total	Control	Treatment	Total	Control	Treatment	Total	Control	Treatment
Balance on Closed Accounts	8,293	7,559	8,872	8,293	7,559	8,872	8,293	7,559	8,872
Balance on Installment Accounts	11,135	11,400	10,908	11,135	11,400	10,908	11,135	11,400	10,908
Number of Student Loans	1.6	1.7	1.5	1.6	1.7	1.5	1.6	1.7	1.5
Balance on Student Loans	10,331	10,127	10,508	10,331	10,127	10,508	10,331	10,127	10,508
Number of Revolving Accounts	3.5	4.2	2.7	3.5	4.2	2.7	3.5	4.2	2.7
Number of Installment Accounts	3.5	3.8	3.2	3.5	3.8	3.2	3.5	3.8	3.2
Number of Mortgages	0.2	0.3	0.1	0.2	0.3	0.1	0.2	0.3	0.1
Number of Open Accounts	0.7	0.8	0.7	0.7	0.8	0.7	0.7	0.8	0.7
Number of Auto Loans	0.2	0.2	0.2	0.2	0.2	0.2	0.2	0.2	0.2
Number of Credit Cards	0.9	1.0	0.8	0.9	1.0	0.8	0.9	1.0	0.8
Number of Lines of Credit	0.1	0.1	0.1	0.1	0.1	0.1	0.1	0.1	0.1
Number of Sales Contracts	0.1	0.1	0.1	0.1	0.1	0.1	0.1	0.1	0.1
Number of Secured Accounts	0.1	0.0	0.1	0.1	0.0	0.1	0.1	0.0	0.1
Number of Unsecured Accounts	0.1	0.1	0.2	0.1	0.1	0.2	0.1	0.1	0.2
Number of Bankruptcies	0.1	0.1	0.1	0.1	0.1	0.1	0.1	0.1	0.1
Tax Liens	2507	3237	1646	2507	3237	1646	2507	3237	1646

Appendix A-2: Indices Created

Alternative Financial Services Index: *Mean(StDev)=0.0235 (.679); Alpha=0.445.* 4 questions measuring the frequency of use of an alternative financial instrument on a 0 to 4 scale. They include pawn loans, payday loans, check cashers, and money orders. The reliability statistic is below general conventions (alpha>0.8).

Financial Plan Index: *Mean (StDev)=0.0153(.677); Alpha=0.7248.* questions asking whether or not the person has taken concrete steps to improve their financial position in the past 6 months. Examples include viewing their credit report, creating a debt payment plan, using a savings program.

Financial Confidence Index: *Mean(St Dev)= -.0155(.738); Alpha=0.8987.* 10 questions measuring the level of success with positive financial behaviors, and level of confidence with financial issues, each on a 1 to 5 scale. For example, budgeting and self-control, paying bills on time, confidence in planning ability.

Appendix A-3: First Stage IV Estimates

The results of the first stage regression are shown below (with covariates suppressed).

	Attended FEC
Counseling Group	0.364***
	(0.000)
Observations	1034

Appendix A-4: Percent Missing Data by Period

Percent Missing Data (relative to full study population)			
	Baseline	6 Months	12 Months
Survey	15%	42%	52%
CR Report	15%	3%	4%
CR Score	53%	55%	55%
Bank Data	*not applicable*		68%

Note: Monthly bank data collected at 12 months for prior 12 months.

Appendix B: Comparison of Sample Demographics to US Population and Population in Poverty

We compare the AFCO pilot population to the total US population, as well as the subset of Americans living in poverty in order to provide context for the group of people studied through this program.

	AFCO Pilot Sample[18]	People in Poverty	Total Population
Married[19]	8.5.%	16.7%	39.6%
Average number of children	1.54	1.56	1.04
Black or African American	63%	23.6%	12.8%
Homeless/Shelter (on a given night)[20]	19.8%[21]	1.41%	0.22%
Homeless/Shelter (at least once in last year)	-	3.44%	0.53%

This comparison again highlights how the participants in the AFCO pilot come from a very select population. Along each dimension, the AFCO participants are considerably further removed from the total population than is the impoverished population. The differences in the rates of self-reported homelessness among study members compared to national estimates of the homeless population are quite stark. While the AFCO population does appear to be quite special, it is also likely of particular interest to policymakers due to its vulnerability.

---

[18] AFCO sample data are taken from table 4 and baseline survey data, combining the treatment and control groups, and excluding the "Not Reported" category.

[19] Estimates of the percentages married, Black or African American, and average number of children taken from the 2012 Current Population Survey.

[20] Estimates of the homeless population taken from the 2010 Annual Homeless Assessment Report to Congress prepared by the Department of Housing and Urban Development. Count estimates are converted to rates based upon estimated poverty rates and counts from the 2010 American Community Survey.

[21] The AFCO population only reported their current living situation.

Appendix C: Popular Community Bank Checking Account and ID Requirements

Totally Free Checking® Account Terms
- This is a free non-interest bearing checking account
- There is no minimum balance requirement
- There is no monthly fee, but prior to the summer of 201?, the account required five or more transactions per month. After that date, there was no minimum number of transactions.
- Automatic opt-out for overdraft
- Free ATM card
- Free unlimited in-network ATM transactions at BPNA and Allpoint ATMs
- Free access to Popular Online Banking
- Free online bill pay
- Free unlimited check writing
- Free online check images
- Free images of paid checks included in your statement
- Money accessible 24/7 – with ATM/MasterCard debit card, Popular online banking and telephone banking
- Customers must fund the account within 30 days of account opening (this payment may be made through direct deposit)
- There is a 3 month (or 90 day) grace period for accounts not meeting the 5 minimum monthly transactions. Customers will be notified that they are not meeting the minimum number of transactions. If this persists beyond the grace period, the account will be converted to Popular's fee-based basic checking account ($5 per month; $3 per month in NY).
- Note: The Parks Opportunity Program participants are New York City employees and should be eligible for the account terms affiliated with New York City Direct Deposit program (e.g., waive the $25 required to open account)

Identification Requirements
- Current (non-expired) and valid government-issued photo identification from most countries, such as a passport, state ID, or Matricula Consular. A current New York State electronic benefit transfer (EBT) card is also an acceptable form of ID.
- Proof of address, such as a voter card or a gas, electricity, or phone bill
- Social Security Number (SSN) or Individual Taxpayer Identification Number (ITIN) needed; actual card is not required

Appendix D: Survey Instruments

1) Baseline survey
2) Follow-up survey

City of New York
Parks & Recreation

SURVEY ABOUT FINANCES

BACKGROUND INFORMATION

1. Last Name:	2. First Name:	3. Date of Birth:

4. Are you of Hispanic or Latino origin?
☐ Yes
☐ No
☐ Prefer not to answer

5. Race: *(select one or more)*
☐ White
☐ Black/African-American
☐ Asian
☐ Native Hawaiian or other Pacific Islander
☐ American Indian or Alaska Native
☐ Prefer not to answer

6. Living Situation:
☐ Rent
☐ Own
☐ Staying with family/friends
☐ Public housing
☐ Homeless/shelter
☐ Prefer not to answer

7. Marital Status:
☐ Married
☐ Single (never married)
☐ Divorced/Separated
☐ Widowed
☐ Prefer not to answer

8. How many adults (18 and over), including yourself, are in your household?

_____

9. How many children (under 18) are in your household?

_____

USE OF FINANCIAL SERVICES

10. Did you have a bank account in the month before starting POP?

☐ No account   ☐ Yes, savings account

☐ Yes, checking account   ☐ Yes, both checking and savings account

12. Did you have any of the following in the month before starting POP? *(check all that apply)*
☐ Prepaid card
☐ Payroll card
☐ EBT/Public Benefits card
☐ Direct deposit to bank account
☐ Direct deposit to payroll card

13. Have you used any of the following in the last month? *(check all that apply)*
☐ Check-cashers
☐ Money orders
☐ Online bill pay
☐ Pay day lender
☐ Pawn shops

11. If you did not have a bank account in the month before starting POP, did you have one in the past?

☐ Yes   ☐ No

➢ **11a. IF YES, why did you close it?** *(check all that apply)*
☐ I could not maintain the minimum balance
☐ Fees were too high
☐ I don't like dealing with banks
☐ I don't trust banks
☐ I had a negative experience with my bank
☐ I have judgments/liens
☐ It was frozen / garnished

☐ Other reason: _____

_____

➢ **11b. IF NO, why don't you have a bank account?** *(check all)*
☐ I can't maintain the minimum balance
☐ Fees are too high
☐ I tried but bank denied me
☐ I don't have the required identification
☐ I don't like dealing with banks
☐ I don't trust banks
☐ I had a negative experience with my bank
☐ I have judgments / liens
☐ I don't want my wages garnished

☐ Other reason: _____

_____

14. If you had an unexpected expense or emergency of $500, how confident are you that you could pay it? ☐ Not at all ☐ A little ☐ Somewhat ☐ Very ☐ Extremely	15. Do you use a budget or spending plan? ☐ Yes ☐ No	16. Have you viewed your credit report in the past 12 months? ☐ Yes ☐ No
	17. Are you saving regularly? ☐ Yes ☐ No 18. Do you have any savings? ☐ Yes ☐ No	19. If you have savings, about how much money do you have saved? $_____
20. About how often do you contribute to savings? ☐ Weekly ☐ Every two weeks ☐ Monthly ☐ Several times a year ☐ Once per year ☐ Less than once per year ☐ Never, do not contribute to savings	21. How often is your household able to pay all bills, such as rent /mortgage, utilities, food, etc? ☐ Almost always ☐ Often ☐ Sometimes ☐ Rarely ☐ Never	22. Do you trust banks? ☐ Not at all ☐ A little ☐ Somewhat ☐ Very ☐ Extremely
23. How much control do you feel over your finances? ☐ No control ☐ A little control ☐ In control ☐ Very in control ☐ Extremely in control	24. How would you rate your understanding of money-management? ☐ Very bad ☐ Poor ☐ Fair ☐ Good ☐ Excellent	25. How frequently do you pay your bills on time? ☐ Almost always ☐ Often ☐ Sometimes ☐ Rarely ☐ Never

OMB Control #1505-0242

 City of New York
Parks & Recreation

Parks Opportunity
Program Survey

 Department of Consumer Affairs
Office of Financial Empowerment

The U.S. Department of the Treasury has asked us to evaluate the financial services provided by the Parks Opportunity Program. To improve this program and provide better services in the future we need your help. Please complete the survey today and return it in the stamped envelope provided. Thank you!

---

1. The first questions are about your experiences looking for employment.

Have you found employment outside of the Parks Opportunity Program?

○ Yes, full-time or more
○ Yes, part time
○ No

---

2. Since starting the Parks Opportunity Program, how many jobs have you...

	0 jobs	1 to 4 jobs	5 to 8 jobs	9 to 12 jobs	13 or more jobs
a. ...applied for?	○	○	○	○	○
b. ...interviewed for?	○	○	○	○	○

---

3. The next questions are about financial counseling.

In the last 6 months, have you attended financial counseling?

○ Yes
○ No ⟶ **Go to question 4**

3a. How much did counseling help your financial situation?

○ Not at all
○ A little
○ Somewhat
○ A lot
○ Extremely

3b. How many counseling sessions did you attend?

○ One
○ Two
○ Three
○ Four
○ Five or more

4. The next questions are about financial goals.

Do you currently have at least one financial goal?

- ○ Yes
- ○ No ⟶ Go to question 5

4a. What is your main financial goal?

[   ]

4b. In the next year, how confident are you that you will be able to achieve this financial goal?

- ○ Not at all confident
- ○ A little confident
- ○ Somewhat confident
- ○ Very confident
- ○ Certain

5. Next we ask about banking.

Do you currently have a checking or savings account?

- ○ Yes, both checking and savings account
- ○ Yes, checking account
- ○ Yes, savings account
- ○ No

6. How often do you....

	Never	Less than once a month	One or more times a month	One or more times a week	About every day
a. ...make a withdrawal or deposit at a bank branch?	○	○	○	○	○
b. ...make a withdrawal or deposit at an ATM?	○	○	○	○	○
c. ...use a debit card to make a purchase?	○	○	○	○	○
d. ...write a check?	○	○	○	○	○
e. ...transfer money or pay bills online?	○	○	○	○	○
f. ...use a mobile phone to access a bank or credit union account?	○	○	○	○	○

7. Do you have any frozen savings or checking accounts?

- ○ Yes
- ○ No
- ○ Not sure

8. Thinking about both active accounts and frozen accounts, at how many different banks or credit unions do you have accounts?

○ None
○ One
○ Two
○ Three
○ More than three
○ Not sure

9. How much do you trust banks and credit unions?

○ Not at all
○ A little
○ Somewhat
○ A lot
○ Extremely

10. The next questions are about direct deposit.

Currently, do you receive your paycheck through direct deposit?

○ Yes, into a bank account at Banco Popular
○ Yes, into an account at another bank or credit union, not Banco Popular
○ Yes, onto a prepaid card
○ No
○ Not sure

11. If you are offered direct deposit at your next job, will you sign up for it?

○ No. Please tell us why: [   ]

○ Yes. Please tell us why: [   ]

12. Thinking about direct deposit compared to a paper paycheck, how much harder or easier does it make each of the following?

	Much harder	Somewhat harder	Slightly harder	About the same	Slightly easier	Somewhat easier	Much easier
a. Accessing your money	○	○	○	○	○	○	○
b. Keeping your money safe	○	○	○	○	○	○	○
c. Saving time	○	○	○	○	○	○	○
d. Saving money	○	○	○	○	○	○	○
e. Paying bills	○	○	○	○	○	○	○
f. Managing your money day-to-day	○	○	○	○	○	○	○

13. The next questions are about prepaid cards and other financial services.

Have you ever had…

	Yes	No	Not sure
a. … a prepaid card?	○	○	○
b. …direct deposit of your paycheck to a prepaid card?	○	○	○
c. …direct deposit of your paycheck into a bank account?	○	○	○

14. Have you ever used a prepaid or payment card to receive…

	Yes	No	Not sure
a. …unemployment benefits?	○	○	○
b. …child support?	○	○	○
c. …public benefits, like EBT, for example?	○	○	○

15. Currently, do you have one or more prepaid cards?

○ Yes

○ No

○ Not sure

16. In the last 30 days, how often have you…

	0 times	1 time	2 to 3 times	4 or more times
a. …used a check cashing store?	○	○	○	○
b. …taken out a pawn shop loan?	○	○	○	○
c. …received an advance loan from a credit card or payday lender?	○	○	○	○
d. …purchased a money order?	○	○	○	○
e. …paid bills online?	○	○	○	○
f. …overdrawn a checking or savings account?	○	○	○	○
g. …paid non-sufficient funds fees, or NSF fees, for overdrawing a bank account?	○	○	○	○
h. …borrowed money from friends or family?	○	○	○	○

17. The next questions are about savings. Please include any savings you may have at home, with family or friends, at a bank or credit union, in a savings program, or any other place.

Currently, about how much money do you have saved?

○ $0

○ $1-$500

○ $501-$1,000

○ $1,001-$1,500

○ $1,501-$2,000

○ More than $2,000

18. About how often do you contribute to savings?

○ Weekly
○ Every two weeks
○ Monthly
○ Several times a year
○ Once per year
○ Less than once per year
○ Never, do not contribute to savings

19. The next questions are about managing your money, credit, and debt.

In the last 6 months, have you...

	Yes	No	Not sure
a. ...signed up for a savings program?	○	○	○
b. ...started saving or increased the amount you regularly save?	○	○	○
c. ...reduced your total debt?	○	○	○
d. ...reviewed your credit report?	○	○	○
e. ...created a plan to pay off debt?	○	○	○
f. ...worked to establish credit using a product such as a secured credit card or a credit builder loan?	○	○	○
g. ...filed for bankruptcy?	○	○	○

20. How would you rate your understanding of money-management?

○ Very bad
○ Poor
○ Fair
○ Good
○ Excellent

21. How would you rate your personal credit record?

○ Very poor
○ Poor
○ Fair
○ Good
○ Excellent

○ Don't know

22. In the next month, how confident are you that you could come up with $500 if an unexpected need arose?

○ Not at all
○ A little
○ Somewhat
○ Very
○ Extremely

23. In the next month, if you were facing a $500 unexpected expense, how would you get the money you need?

- ○ Borrow or ask for help from friends or family
- ○ Take out a pay day loan or pawn something you own
- ○ Use savings
- ○ Work more
- ○ Use a credit card
- ○ Sell something you own
- ○ I would not be able to access this money
- ○ Other place. Please tell us: [   ]

24. How worried are you about your finances?

- ○ Not at all
- ○ A little
- ○ Somewhat
- ○ Very
- ○ Extremely

25. Currently, how successful are you at...

	Not at all	A little	Somewhat	Very	Extremely
a. ...controlling your spending?	○	○	○	○	○
b. ...paying your bills on time?	○	○	○	○	○
c. ...planning for your financial future?	○	○	○	○	○
d. ...providing for yourself and your family?	○	○	○	○	○
e. ...saving money?	○	○	○	○	○

26. Thinking about the way you spend your money....

	Not at all	A Little	Somewhat	Very	Extremely
a. ...how confident are you making decisions about money?	○	○	○	○	○
b. ...how confident are you that the way you manage money will affect your future?	○	○	○	○	○
c. ...how much in debt do you consider yourself?	○	○	○	○	○

...how often do you...	Never	Rarely	Sometimes	Often	Very often
e. ...keep track of all of your expenses?	○	○	○	○	○
f. ...compare prices when you shop?	○	○	○	○	○
g. ...use a budget or spending plan?	○	○	○	○	○

27. In the last 30 days, how often did you feel that you were not able to control the important things in your life?

○ Never
○ Rarely
○ Sometimes
○ Often
○ Very often

28. Next we ask about your household.

In the last month, what was your households' total monthly take-home income from each of the following sources?

	$0	$1-$500	$501-$1,000	$1,001-$1,500	$1,501-$2,000	More than $2,000
a. Employment, including work for someone else, self-employment, or any work for pay.	○	○	○	○	○	○
b. Public benefits, such as cash assistance, Social Security, Disability, Unemployment, rental or housing assistance, child care, and food stamps.	○	○	○	○	○	○
c. Other sources. Please tell us:	○	○	○	○	○	○

29. In the last 6 months, has your household experienced an unexpected drop in income or an unexpected expense of at least $500?

○ Yes
○ No

30. Currently, how many adults <u>18 years of age or older</u> live in your household?

[   ] Adults

31. Currently, how many children <u>under the age of 18</u> live in your household?

[   ] Children

32. Currently, what is your living situation?

○ Shelter, transitional housing, or homeless
○ Own
○ Rent, but not public housing
○ Public housing
○ Staying with family or friends

33. Finally, we ask for your opinion on financial matters.

How much is your decision whether or not to save money in a savings or checking account affected by…

	Not at all	A little	Somewhat	A lot	Extremely
a. …eligibility for public benefits?	○	○	○	○	○
b. …the risk of garnishment due to outstanding debt you may have?	○	○	○	○	○

34. Do you think the amount of money a person saves in a savings or checking account can affect their eligibility for…

	Definitely not	It depends	Yes, certainly	Not sure
a. …Temporary Assistance for Needy Families, or TANF?	○	○	○	○
b. …Food stamps, Supplemental Nutrition Assistance Program, or SNAP?	○	○	○	○
c. …Medicaid, excluding Medicaid for the elderly, blind or disabled?	○	○	○	○

35. Imagine you win $1,000 in the lottery today.

a. Would you rather wait 6 weeks for the full $1,000 or take $850 now?

○ Take $850 today
○ Wait 6 weeks for $1,000

b. Would you rather wait 6 weeks for the full $1,000 or take $900 now?

○ Take $900 today
○ Wait 6 weeks for $1,000

c. Would you rather wait 6 weeks for the full $1,000 or take $950 now?

○ Take $950 today
○ Wait 6 weeks for $1,000

Thank you very much for taking the time to complete this survey.

Please return the completed survey in the postage-paid envelope provided to:
Sterling Hall, Room B607
475 North Charter Street
Madison, WI 53706-1582